FACES in Art

Words that appear in **bold** type are defined in the glossary on pages 28 and 29.

Please visit our web site at: **www.garethstevens.com**
**For a free color catalog describing Gareth Stevens Publishing's
list of high-quality books and multimedia programs, call
1-800-542-2595 (USA) or 1-800-387-3178 (Canada).
Gareth Stevens Publishing's fax: (414) 332-3567.**

Library of Congress Cataloging-in-Publication Data

Baumbusch, Brigitte.
   Faces in art / by Brigitte Baumbusch.
      p. cm. — (What makes a masterpiece?)
   Includes index.
   ISBN 0-8368-4378-9 (lib. bdg.)
   1. Faces in art—Juvenile literature. I. Title. II. Series.
   N7573.3.B379713   2004
   704.9'42—dc22   2004045384

This edition first published in 2005 by
Gareth Stevens Publishing
A World Almanac Education Group Company
330 West Olive Street, Suite 100
Milwaukee, Wisconsin 53212 USA

Copyright © Andrea Dué s.r.l. 1999

This U.S. edition copyright © 2005 by Gareth Stevens, Inc.
Additional end matter copyright © 2005 by Gareth Stevens, Inc.

Translator: Erika Pauli

Gareth Stevens series editor: Dorothy L. Gibbs
Gareth Stevens art direction: Tammy West

Printed in the United States of America

1 2 3 4 5 6 7 8 9 08 07 06 05 04

What Makes a ? Masterpiece?

FACES
in Art

by Brigitte Baumbusch

GARETH**STEVENS**
GS
PUBLISHING
A World Almanac Education Group Company

What makes a face . . .

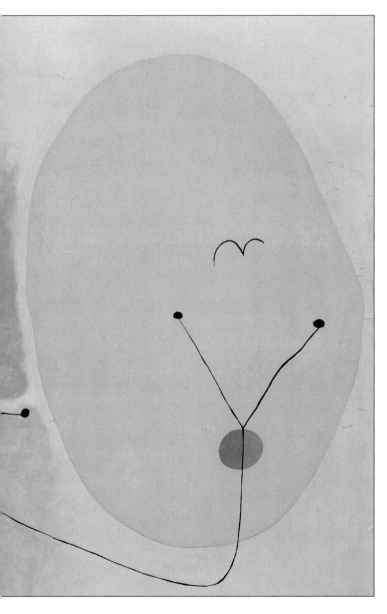

This egg-shaped face was painted in 1938 by Spanish artist Joan Miró.

Sometimes, an Easter egg has a face, too.

4

A face can be cut into a **hollowed out** pumpkin — like Charlie Brown's "Great Pumpkin."

The face on this "bushy head" was made by **pleating** the dried **husks** of Indian corn. It is a mask used by the Seneca Indians of North America.

a masterpiece?

Faces can be simple.

The plain face in **relief** on this small **bronze plaque** comes from Sicily. It is very old. In fact, it is more than 2,700 years old!

This **portrait** of a woman is by Pablo Picasso, another famous Spanish artist, and it was painted the same year as the portrait on page 4, by Joan Miró.

Faces can be complex.

Some faces are big.

This enormous face is on a **sculpture** carved from **basalt**. The sculpture is the head of an Olmec king. The Olmec people lived thousands of years ago in the part of Central America that is now Mexico.

These little faces are on heads made of colored glass. Each head is a **charm** that was worn on a necklace. These charms were made by the Phoenicians. They were **merchant** people from **ancient** times who sailed the Mediterranean Sea.

Some faces are small.

Some faces are round.

This face is painted on a round piece of **terra-cotta** pottery. The pottery is a type of water bottle made by many South American peoples.

The thin face on this portrait of a woman is the work of artist and sculptor Amedeo Modigliani. Although he was Italian, Modigliani lived in Paris in the early 1900s, which is when this portrait was painted.

Other faces are long.

This face is famous.

The "Mona Lisa," by Italian **Renaissance master** Leonardo da Vinci, is one of the most famous portraits in the world. It hangs in the Louvre, in Paris, which is one of the largest museums in the world.

This small face dates back to the Stone Age. It is on the head of a lady that was carved about 20,000 years ago from the tusk of a **mammoth**.

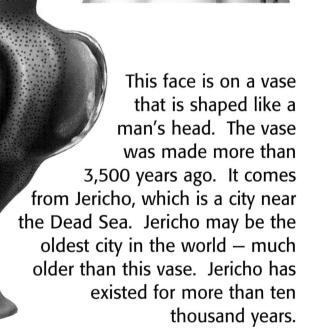

This face is on a vase that is shaped like a man's head. The vase was made more than 3,500 years ago. It comes from Jericho, which is a city near the Dead Sea. Jericho may be the oldest city in the world — much older than this vase. Jericho has existed for more than ten thousand years.

These are nameless.

Faces can be serious.

This portrait of Sigmund Freud, a famous Austrian doctor, was painted by modern American artist Ben Shahn. Sigmund Freud was an expert in **interpreting** dreams.

Leonardo da Vinci not only painted famous masterpieces such as the "Mona Lisa" but also drew **caricatures**. This trio (above) is part of a larger work called "Seven **Grotesque** Heads."

The laughing face on the handle of this stick is a jester. A jester's job was to make people laugh. Jesters were much like today's **comedians**.

Faces can be funny.

Some faces are happy.

The smiling face of this beautiful lady was carved in
ivory. This sculpture may be the portrait of a queen.
It was found in the ancient Assyrian town of Nimrud.
About three thousand years ago, the kingdom of Assyria
stretched from the Tigris River to the Mediterranean Sea,
in the area that, today, is modern Iraq and Syria.

The young woman in this painting is **Saint** Mary Magdalene, from the Bible. She is weeping in sorrow for her **sins**. Caravaggio, the Italian artist who painted her, was not very well-liked in his time because he used ordinary people as models for holy saints.

Some faces are sad.

Sometimes, faces are out of place.

People in the Middle Ages were fond of imagining monsters, like the creature in this relief sculpture. It is a man with his face on his chest!

Sixteenth-century Italian artist Giuseppe Arcimboldo painted amusing faces made of flowers, fruits and vegetables, animals, books, and many other objects.

As a joke, he painted a picture of a vegetable basket (above), which, turned upside down, becomes a face (right).

Sometimes,
they are hidden.

Faces change with age.

"The Three Ages of Man" is a portrait of the same man as a child, a young man, and an old man. It was painted by Giorgione, a great Italian painter of the Renaissance.

Faces change with feelings.

The faces in this early nineteenth-century painting show a variety of feelings, or emotions. The artist was Frenchman Louis-Léopold Boilly.

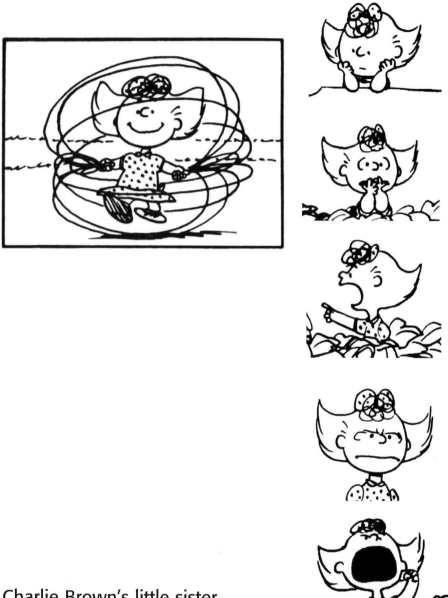

Charlie Brown's little sister,
Sally, has a very expressive face.
It is easy to tell if she is happy,
thoughtful, embarrassed, upset,
angry, or furious.

Animals have faces, too.

This **striking** bronze-and-silver tiger's head is an example of Chinese art. It was made more than two thousand years ago.

This painting from 1911 (opposite page) is called "I and the Village." It shows life in the Russian countryside. In the **foreground**, you see the faces of a man and a cow looking at each other. The artist was Marc Chagall. Although born in Russia, Chagall is usually considered a French painter because his most famous work was done in France, after he moved there in 1910. He also lived for a while in the United States.

Some cars even look as if they have faces.

This toy made in the 1950s is a model
of an American car — the Pontiac Star Chief.

The faces of houses are called façades.

These houses were painted more than one hundred years ago by Frenchman Henri Rousseau, who was known as "le Douanier," or "the **Customs** Officer," because that is what he did for a living. Rousseau was not a professional artist. He painted because it was what he liked to do best.

GLOSSARY

ancient
relating to a time early in history, from the earliest civilizations until about the time of the Roman Empire

basalt
a kind of rock, formed when hot lava from volcanoes cools. Basalt is a hard, heavy rock that is dark gray to black in color

bronze
a hard metal alloy (combination of two or more metals) that is a mixture of mainly copper and tin

caricatures
drawings or sketches of people, which distort or exaggerate certain physical features and characteristics

charm
a small trinket or ornament, often the miniature of a real-life animal or object, worn on a bracelet, necklace, or some kind of chain as a piece of jewelry

comedians
entertainers who try to make people laugh by telling funny stories or by performing funny actions or activities

Customs
a government agency that regulates a country's imports and exports and collects the appropriate fees, called duties or tolls

foreground
the part of a picture or scene that is closest to the front or nearest the viewer

grotesque
having an extemely unusual, unnatural, absurd, or bizarre appearance

hollowed out
having had the insides removed, creating a cavity, or empty space

husks
the leaflike pods or outside layers covering certain types of fruits and seeds, especially the covering on an ear of corn

interpreting
explaining confusing language, events, or ideas in an understandable way

mammoth
an extinct prehistoric, elephantlike animal with long, upward-curving tusks and a lot of hair on its body

master
a well-known artist who has reached the highest level of skill and whose work is considered a model or ideal

merchant
a person whose work, or business, is buying, selling, and trading to earn a living, historically, traveling great distances to find and deliver goods

plaque
a flat piece of wood, metal, or another material that usually contains some kind of ornament or design and is generally used for decoration

pleating
folding material over onto itself in a continuous pattern

portrait
a picture, photograph, or painting of a person that usually shows just the person's head, neck, and shoulders

relief
a form of sculpture in which the details of the figure or design are raised and stick out from or project above a flat surface

Renaissance
a period of European history, between the Middle Ages (14th century) and modern times (17th century), during which learning flourished and interest in classical (relating to ancient Greek and Roman civilizations) art and literature was renewed, or "reborn"

saint
a human being who is recognized and honored for his or her holiness or virtue

sculpture
a work of art created by carving, modeling, or molding materials such as wood, rock, stone, clay, or metal into a figure or object that is three-dimensional, instead of flat.

sins
thoughts, words, and actions that break religious or moral laws

striking
very beautiful or having other fascinating qualities that attract attention

terra-cotta
brownish-orange earth, or clay, that hardens when it is baked and is often used to make pottery and roofing tiles

PICTURE LIST

page 4 – Joan Miró (1893-1983): Portrait, detail, 1938. Zürich, Kunsthaus. Museum photo. © Joan Miró by SIAE, 1999.

page 5 – Pleated mask of the "Corn Face" or "Bushy Head" society. Iroquois Indians (Seneca) of the State of New York. New York, Museum of the American Indian. Drawing by Lorenzo Cecchi.

The Great Pumpkin from the comic strip "Peanuts" by Charles M. Schulz has been reproduced with the kind permission of Peanuts © United Feature Syndicate, Inc.

page 6 – Bronze plaque with a simplified human face in repoussé. Iron Age, 8th century B.C., from Mendalito di Adrano (Sicily). Syracuse, Archaeological Museum. Drawing by Luigi Ieracitano.

page 7 –Pablo Picasso (1881-1973): Seated Woman, 1938. Private property. Photo Scala Archives. © Pablo Picasso by SIAE, 1999.

page 8 – Colossal head in basalt, known as "The King." Olmec civilization, around 1200 B.C. San Lorenzo, Veracruz (Mexico). Drawing by Lorenzo Cecchi.

page 9 – Small head in colored glass. Carthaginian art, 4th-3rd century B.C.

Cagliari, Archaeological Museum. Drawing by Paola Ravaglia.

page 10 – Terra-cotta vessel reproducing a human face. Nazca civilization (Peru), first centuries A.D. Private property. Drawing by Lorenzo Cecchi.

page 11 – Amedeo Modigliani (1884-1920): Gypsy with a Baby, detail, 1919. Washington, National Gallery of Art, Chester Dale Collection. Museum photo.

page 12 – Leonardo da Vinci (1452-1519): Mona Lisa. Paris, Louvre. Photo Scala Archives.

page 13 – Small head of a woman in mammoth tusk. Gravettian, c. 18,000 B.C., from Brassempouy, Landes (France). Saint-Germain-en-Laye, Musée des Antiquités Nationales. Drawing by Lorenzo Cecchi.

Anthropomorphic vase in terra-cotta. Canaanite art, 18th-17th century B.C., from Jericho. Jerusalem, Israel Museum. Drawing by Lorenzo Cecchi.

page 14 – Ben Shahn (1898-1969): Portrait of Sigmund Freud, 1956. Private property. Photo Scala Archives. © Ben Shahn by SIAE, 1999.

page 15 –Leonardo da Vinci (1452-1519): Seven Grotesque Heads, detail. Venice, Academy. Photo Scala Archives.

Jester's stick in wood. French art of the 15th century. Florence, Bargello Museum. Drawing Studio Stalio / Alessandro Cantucci.

page 16 – Head of a woman in ivory. Assyrian art, 8th century B.C., from Nimrud. Baghdad, Iraq Museum. Drawing Studio Stalio / Alessandro Cantucci.

page 17 – Caravaggio (1571-1610): The Magdalen, detail. Rome, Galleria Doria Pamphilj. Photo Scala Archives.

page 18 – Nicolò (12th century): relief with an imaginary creature. Detail of the jamb of the portal of the cathedral of Ferrara (Italy). Drawing Studio Stalio / Alessandro Cantucci.

page 19 – Giuseppe Arcimboldo (1527-1593): The Gardener. Cremona, Museo Civico. Photo Scala Archives.

pages 20-21 – Giorgione (1477-1510): The Three Ages of Man. Florence, Galleria Palatina, Pitti Palace. Photo Scala Archives.

page 22 – Louis-Léopold Boilly (1761-1845): Study of Thirty-Five Facial Expressions. Tourcoing, Musée des Beaux-Arts. Museum photo.

page 23 – The sequence of various frames of Sally from the comic strip "Peanuts" by Charles M. Schulz has been reproduced with the kind permission of Peanuts © United Feature Syndicate, Inc.

page 24
Marc Chagall (1887-1985): I and the Village, 1911. New York, The Museum of Modern Art. Photo Museum of Modern Art / Scala, 2003. © Marc Chagall by SIAE, 1999.

page 25 – Tiger head in bronze with silver inlay. Chinese art, eastern Chou dynasty, 3rd century B.C. Cologne, Museum für Ostasiatische Kunst. Drawing by Lorenzo Cecchi.

page 26 – Tin toy of 1954 reproducing a Pontiac Star Chief. Yokohama, Teruhisa Kitahara Tin Toy Museum. Drawing by Lorenzo Cecchi.

page 27 – Henri Rousseau (1844-1910): Landscape with Arch and Three Houses, detail. Paris, Musée de l'Orangerie. Photo Scala Archives.

INDEX

animals 25
Arcimboldo, Giuseppe 19
artists 4, 7, 11, 14, 17, 19, 22, 25, 27

Boilly, Louis-Léopold 22

Caravaggio 17
cars 26
Chagall, Marc 25
Charlie Brown 5, 23

da Vinci, Leonardo 12, 15

Giorgione 20

houses 27

masks 5
materials
  basalt 8
  bronze 6, 25
  corn husks 5
  eggs 4
  glass 9
  ivory 16
  pumpkins 5
  silver 25
  terra-cotta 10
  tusks 13

men 13, 18, 20, 25
Middle Ages 18
Miró, Joan 4, 7
Modigliani, Amedeo 11

Olmec people 8

Phoenicians 9
Picasso, Pablo 7
portraits 7, 11, 12, 14, 16, 20
pottery 10

relief 6, 18
Renaissance 12, 20
Rousseau, Henri 27

sculpture 8, 16, 18
Seneca Indians 5
Shahn, Ben 14
shapes
  big 8
  egg-shaped 4
  long 11
  round 10
  small 6, 9, 13

women 7, 11, 17